CW00840543

MY MEN

sexy

/ˈsɛksi/

Saznajte kako izgovarati

adjective

1. 1.

sexually attractive or exciting.

"sexy French underwear"

sinonimi:

sexually attractive, seductive, desirable, alluring, inviting,
sensual, sultry, slinky, provocative, tempting, tantalizing;
nubile, voluptuous, shapely, luscious, lush;
feline;
bedroom;
flirtatious, coquettish;
*informal*hot, fanciable, beddable, come-hither, come-to-
bed;
*informal*fit, peng;
*informal*foxy, cute, bootylicious;
*informal*spunky;
*vulgar slang*fuck-me
"she's so sexy"
erotic, arousing, exciting, stimulating, hot;
sexually explicit, titillating, suggestive, racy, risqué,
provocative, spicy, juicy, adult, X-rated;
rude, coarse, smutty, pornographic, vulgar, crude, lewd,
lubricious;
*informal*raunchy, steamy, naughty, horny, porno, blue,
skin;
*informal*saucy, fruity;
*informal*gamy
"a TV show featuring sexy home videos"

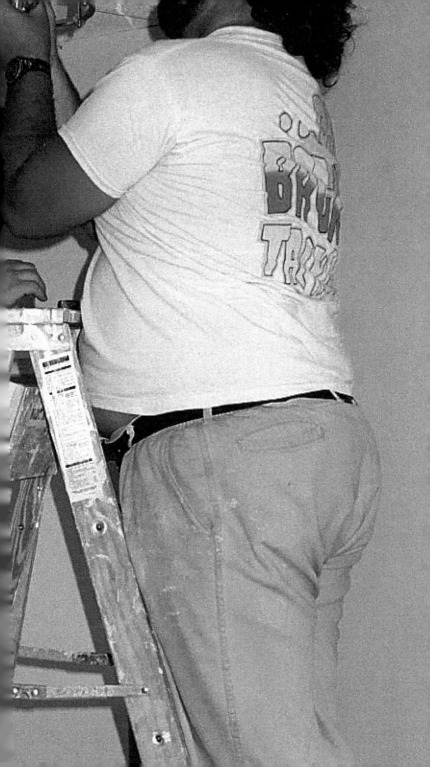

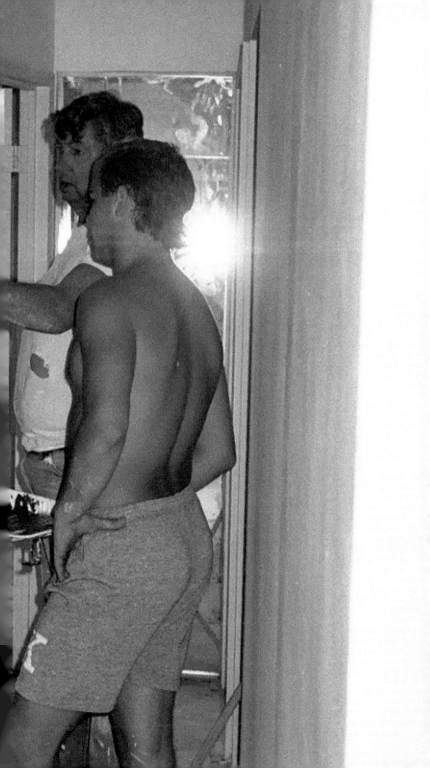

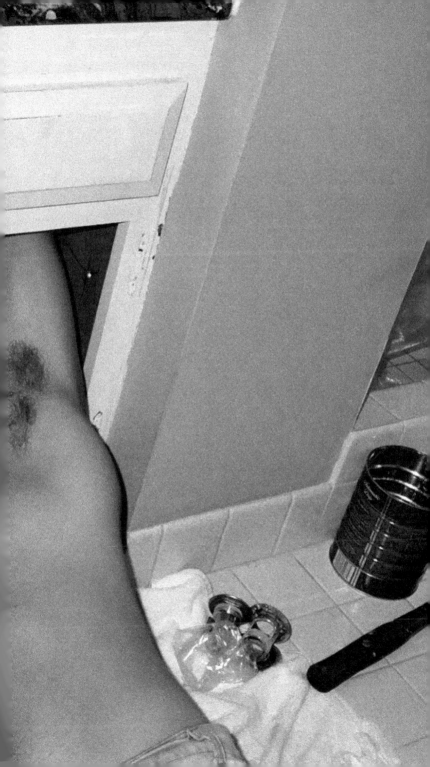

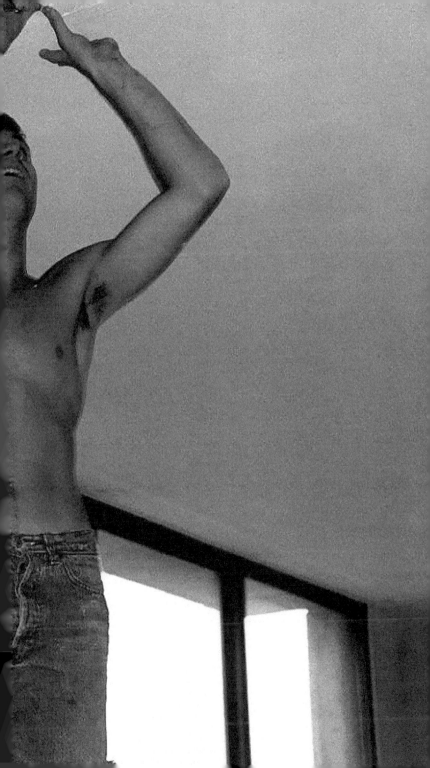

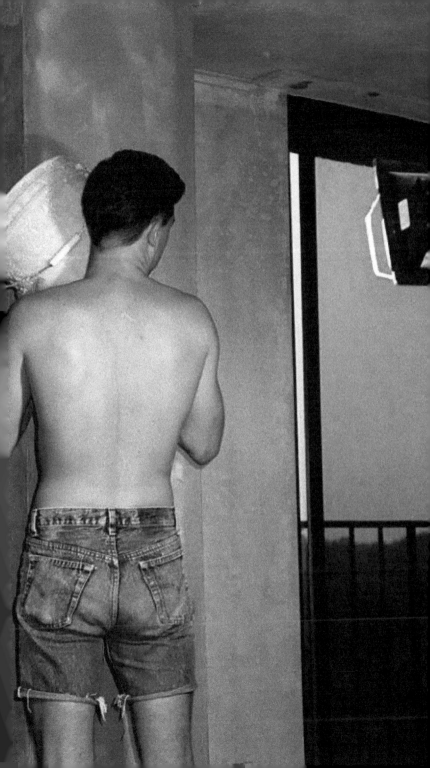

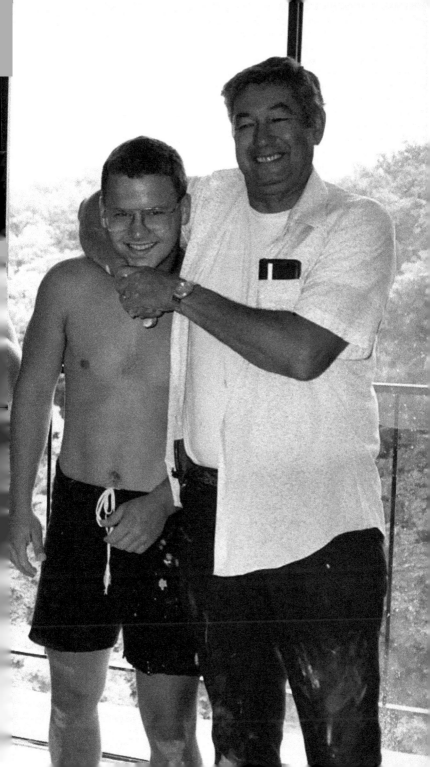

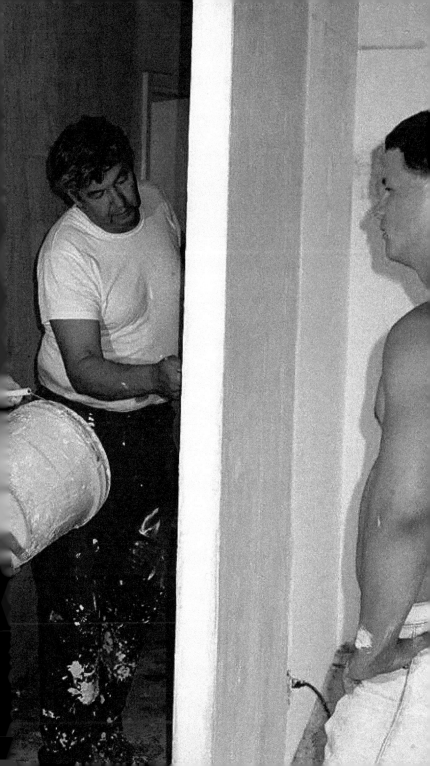

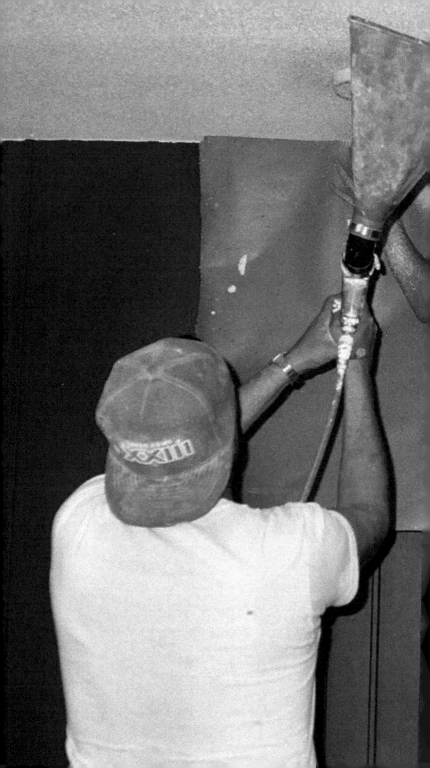

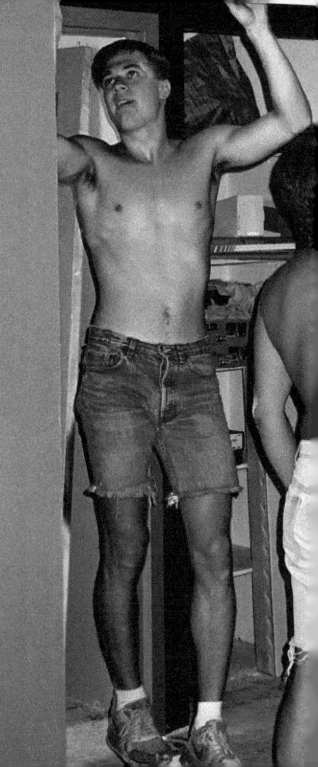

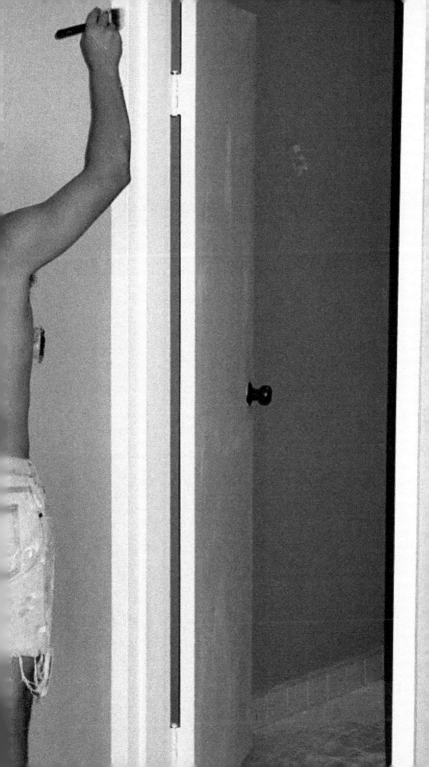

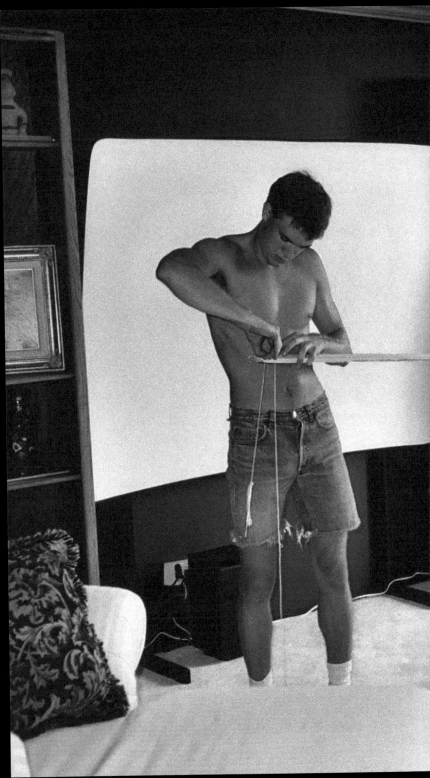

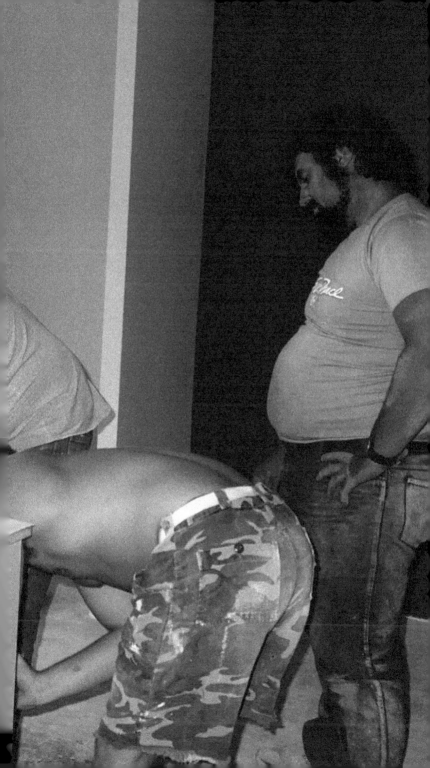

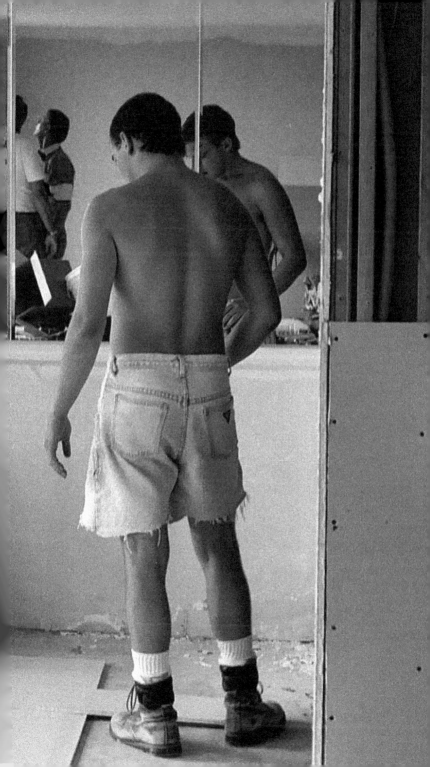

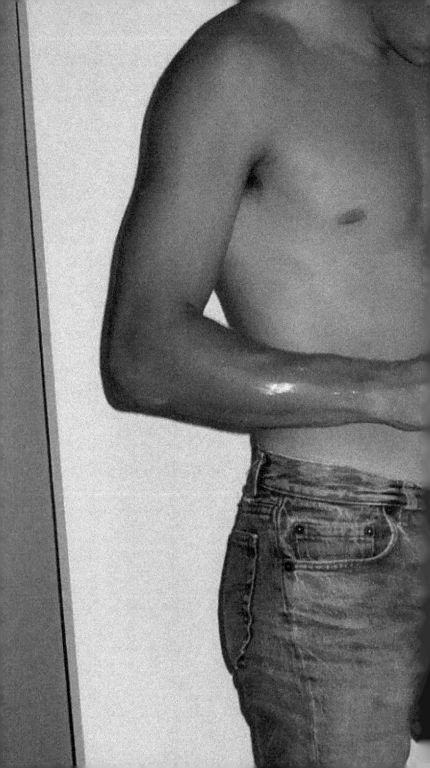

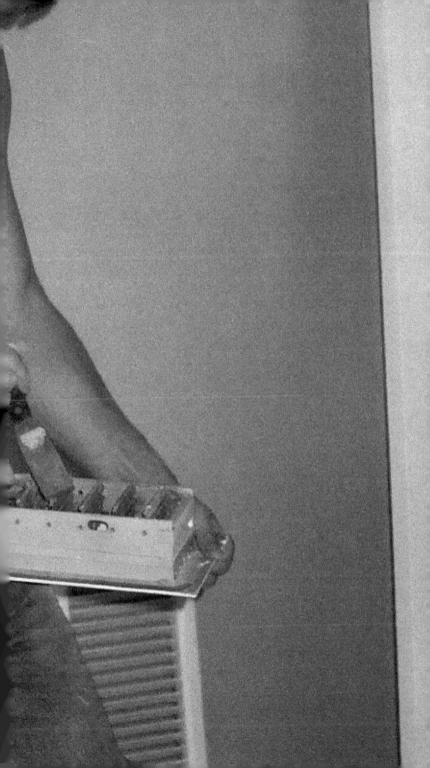

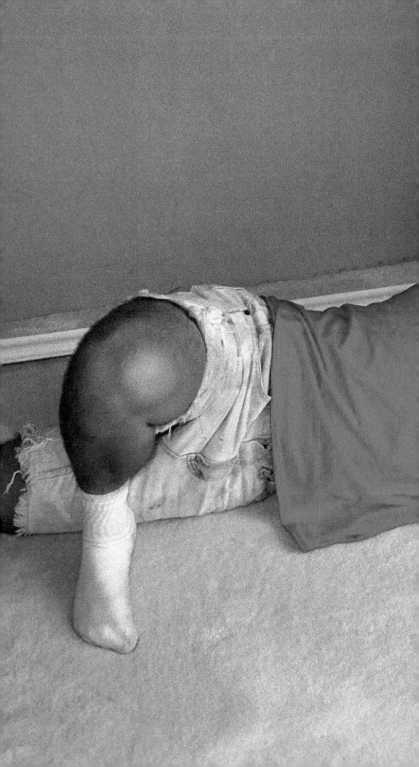